YANNI
Truth Of Touch

ISBN 978-1-4803-3320-8

HAL•LEONARD®
CORPORATION
7777 W. BLUEMOUND RD. P.O. BOX 13819 MILWAUKEE, WI 53213

Visit Hal Leonard Online at
www.halleonard.com

TRUTH OF TOUCH

Music by YANNI
and MIKLOS MALEK

D.S. al Coda

ECHO OF A DREAM

Music by YANNI

2nd time: R.H. 8va

8vb -

(8vb) -

(8vb) -

loco

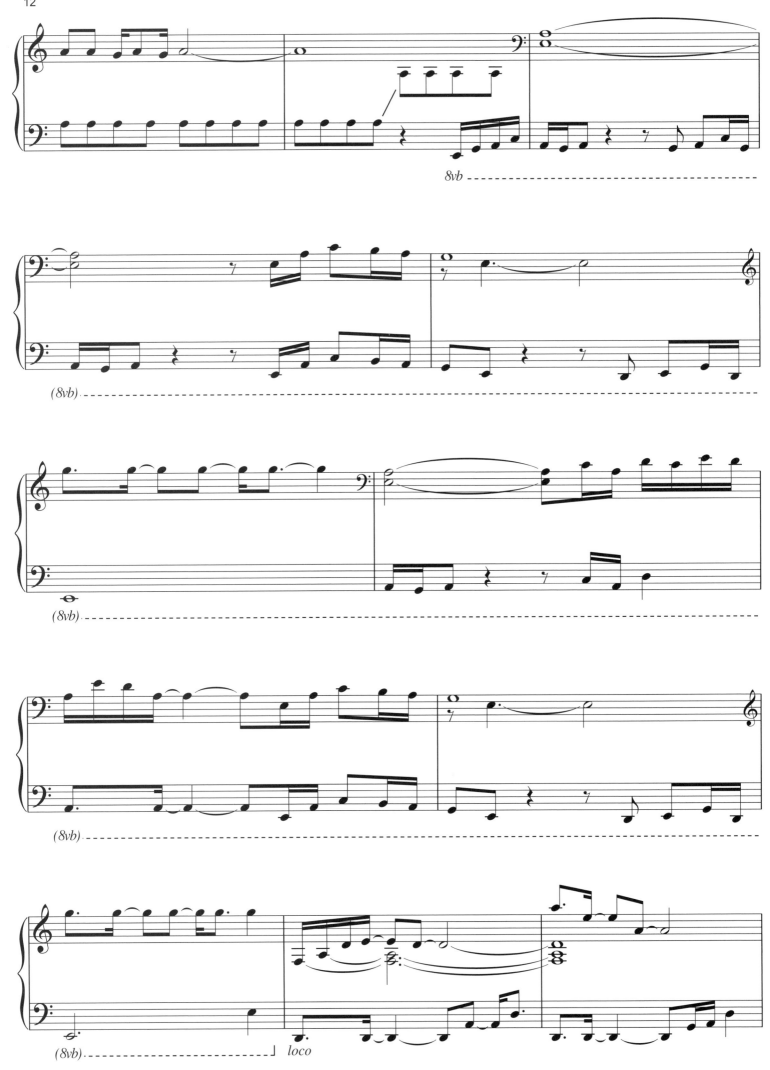

8vb -

(8vb) -

(8vb) -

(8vb) -

(8vb) - ⌐ *loco*

Repeat and Fade

Optional Ending

SEASONS

Music by YANNI
and MIKLOS MALEK

With a Latin flavor

D.S. al Coda

CODA

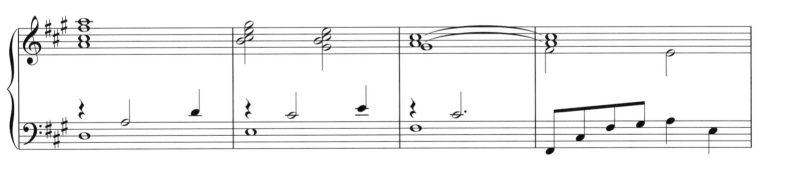

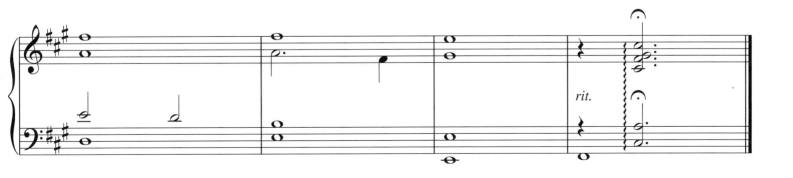

VOYAGE

Music by YANNI
and MIKLOS MALEK

Moderately

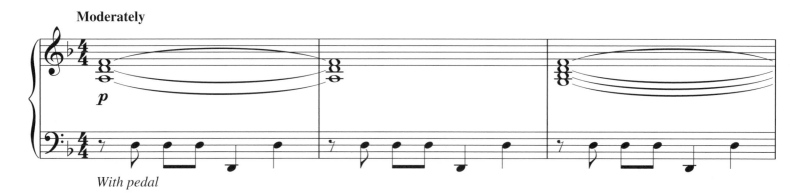

With pedal

FLASH OF COLOR

Music by YANNI
and MIKLOS MALEK

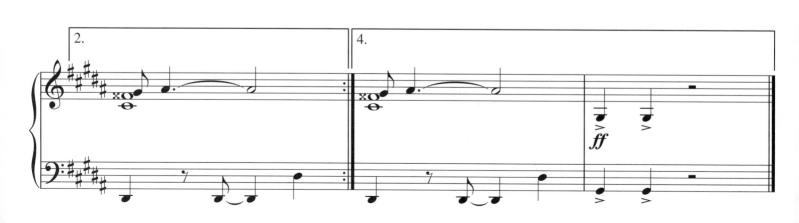

VERTIGO

Music by YANNI
and MIKLOS MALEK

Moderate groove

With pedal

To Coda ⊕

dim.

1.

2.

NINE

Music by YANNI

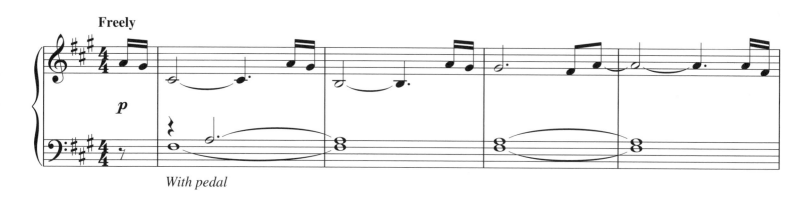

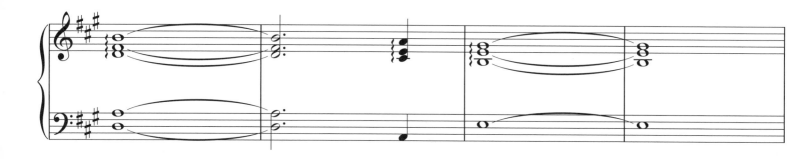

Ambient groove

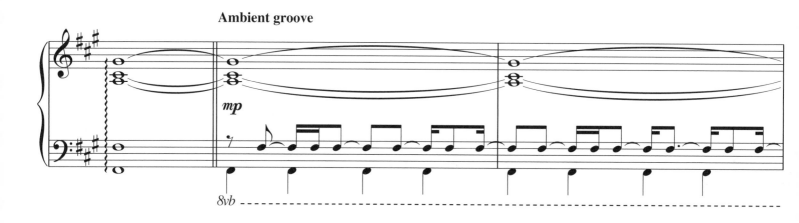

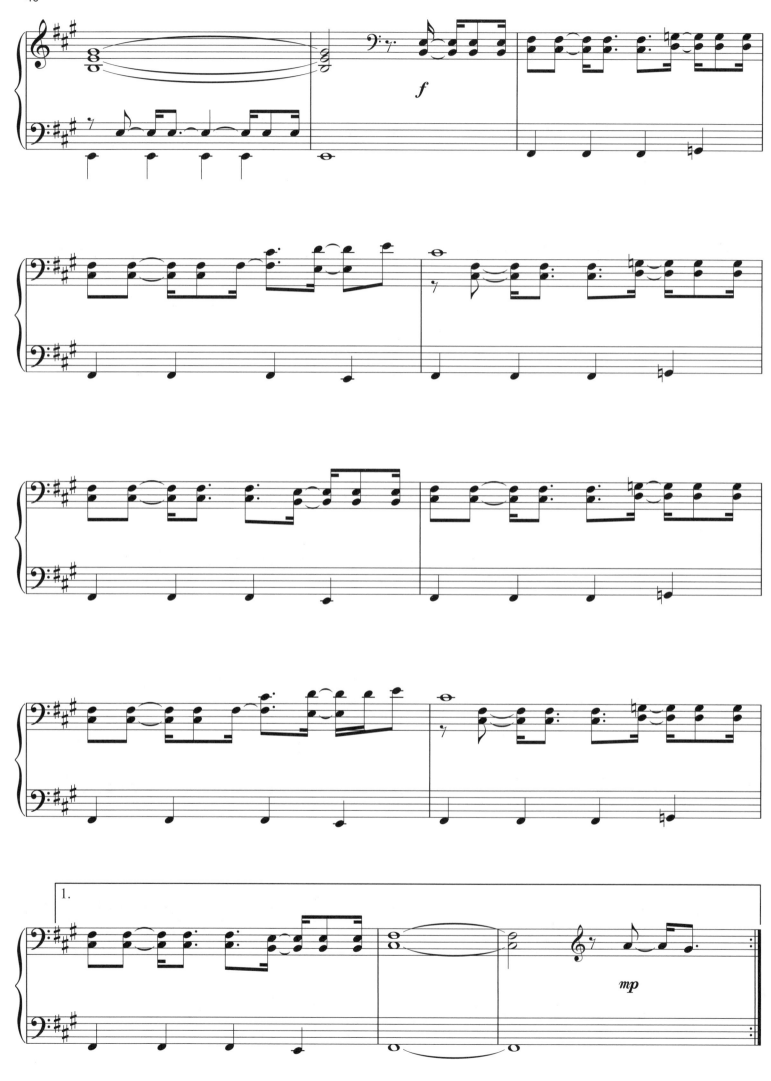

I CAN'T WAIT

Music by LESLIE MILLS and CHRIS PELCER
Lyrics by LESLIE MILLS

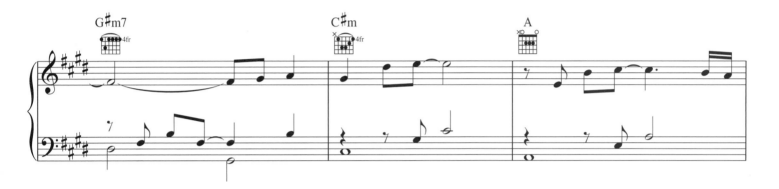

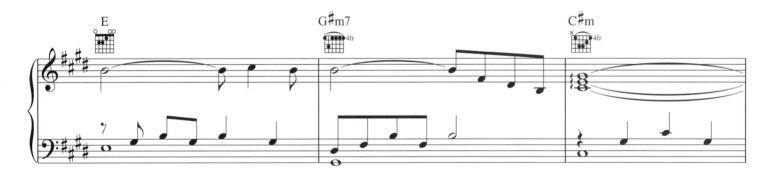

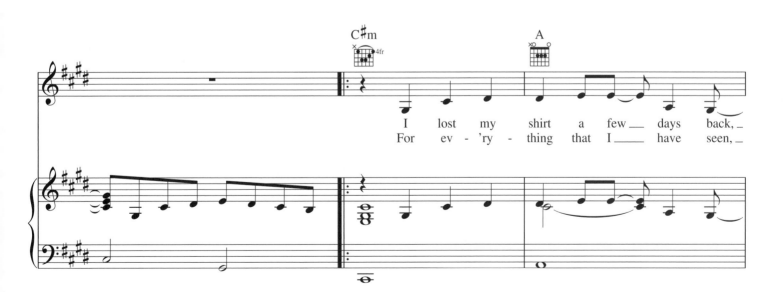

I lost my shirt a few ___ days back, ___
For ev-'ry-thing that I ___ have seen, ___

GUILTY PLEASURE

Music by YANNI
and NAYO

Slow shuffle

mp

With pedal

50

52

O LUCE CHE BRILLA
NELL' OSCURITÀ

Music by YANNI and NATHAN PACHECO
Lyrics by NATHAN PACHECO

Moderately slow

Scen - do - no___ le nu - vo - le o - scu -
Il ___ chias - so del - la gen - te

ran - do la spe - ran - za,
gri - da in - dif - fe - ren - te,

men - tre le stel - le e ___ la
ab - ban - do - na - to ___ al

lu - na ___ sem - bra - no spa - ri - re.
suo - lo, so - lo cer - co la ___ pa - ce. E

I'M SO

Music by YANNI
and ERIC SANICOLA

LONG WAY HOME

Music by LESLIE MILLS
and CHRIS PELCER

Moderately slow

p

With pedal

mp

YANNI & ARTURO

Music by YANNI

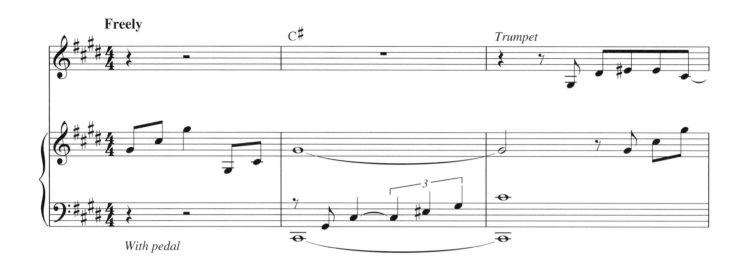

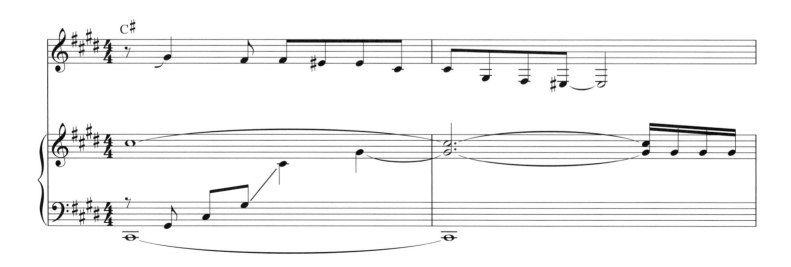

Moderate groove

72

Tpt. as written

Tpt. ad lib.

Tpt. as written

MIST OF A KISS

Music by YANNI

Freely, with motion

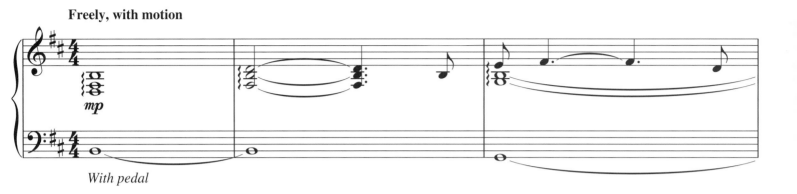

With pedal

Moderate groove

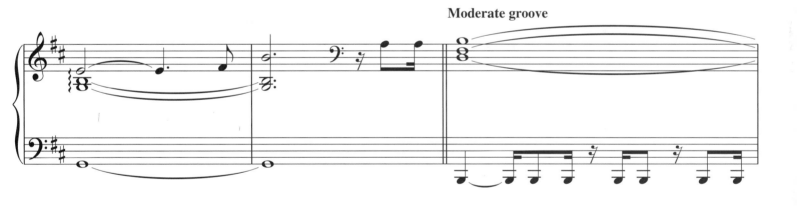

Repeat and Fade

Optional Ending

SECRET

Music by YANNI, CHLOE LOWERY,
MARC RUSSELL and DAVID SCHEUER
Lyrics by CHLOE LOWERY

D.S. al Coda